THE NORTH CAPE

AND ITS HINTERLAND

SIGURD SENJE

THE NORTH CAPE
AND ITS HINTERLAND

TANUM–NORLI

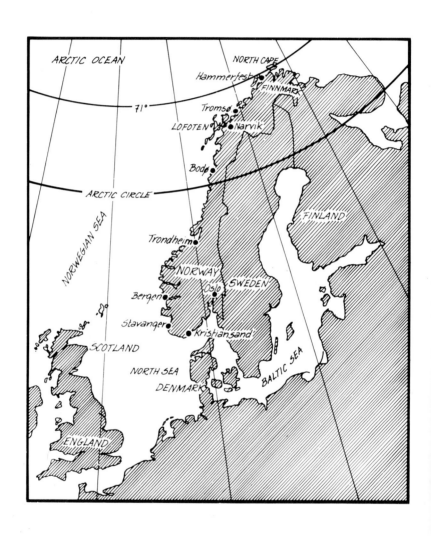

Drawings by Omar Andréen.
Photos by Sigurd Senje, Tore Bredvei, and Kaare A. Krog.
Old photos by courtesy of Nordkapp kommune and Gjesvær skole.

ISBN 82-518-0822-7
Dreyer Aksjeselskap – Stavanger

CONTENTS

Tourists in Honningsvåg.

ONLY A LANDMARK?

Every summer tens of thousands of travellers go north as far as Norway stretches, to pose for a moment on the outermost point of the European map with the Arctic Ocean in the background – preferably with the midnight sun hanging as a shining medal over the horizon.

As a rule the travellers from far away are very busy people; they take some snapshots and turn quickly south again. What have they actually seen? What experience did they have of the natural environment and of the northernmost human community in Europe?

The North Cape is still there when the summer tourists have vanished; it has a permanent population and an everyday life. The people living here experience Europe's northernmost outpost all the year round, not least when the sun stays below the horizon and is not to be seen by day or by night. For ten months of the year these people live their own lives, hidden from any tourist.

This booklet has been written for those travellers who want to know a little more about the people and environment of the North Cape. Come, let's take a closer look at the island called *Magerøy*.

SURROUNDINGS

The North Cape plateau is situated in latitude 71°10'21" North, on the top of steep cliffs that plunge 307 metres down into the Polar Sea.

It is these dramatic mountain formations that have given the North Cape its peculiar character and appeal for seafarers and tourists. No matter that the tiny spit of land called *Knivskjellodden*, a few hundred metres to the west, juts out some 1500 metres farther towards the Pole. The Cape is the eyecatcher and will remain the big attraction.

Anyone coming here for the first time will readily agree on this. Up here on the wide plateau you feel as though you were simultaneously on the roof of the world and at the world's end.

Reindeer grazing at the Cape.

Winter at the fishing station.

This is the final point of your journey. You are on the edge of an abyss, looking down into an ice-cold ocean that extends towards infinity, following the northern arc of the globe. Somewhere over the horizon lie the white, uninhabitable, endless plains of snow around the North Pole.

The name of the island you are visiting, the *Magerøy,* has an origin that suggests *meagre island*, not unfittingly. The land is indeed meagre, for no tree grows here, the earth is not good enough for profitable farming, and no kind of grain will ripen in this climate. Only the reindeer find sufficient food in the grass and moss among the stones.

Yet things are not so bad as you might expect in these latitudes. Nature has given the island a typical coastal climate, with relatively mild winters and temperate summers. The harbours are free of ice even during the worst winter conditions, and the air is surprisingly mild. This is due to the Gulf Stream, which blesses the whole Norwegian coast with warm water from the Caribbean, resulting in an uncommonly temperate climate all the way. On Magerøy, the median temperature in January (c. $-3°$) is twenty degrees Celsius higher than the average for latitude 71 (and fifty higher than in Siberia!) The island has a yearly precipitation of c. 790 mm and around two hundred days of frost and snow.

In winter the sun is down for 67 days, from 19th November to 25th January, while in summer the midnight sun shines for 77 days, from 14th May to 30th July.

The islanders can tell you of sheltered green creeks in contrast to the windy mountain tops. One of these creeks is the *Hornvika* (Horn creek) near the picturesque 'horn' sticking out from the Cape, where the ships anchored in the old days. On a good day you may be surprised by the flowers you find here. But please, don't pick them, the plant life around the Cape is protected. In fact, both the plant and the animal life were protected by law as early as 1929.

About half the island of Magerøy is covered with grass and moss that give good pasture for the reindeer herds, estimated at around five thousand head.

The rocks that surround you on the island are mainly pre-cambrian, granite and slate. An area of limestone rises as a white

The Church Gate with The Horn in the background.

The limestone hill.

A typical steep cliff on Magerøy.

Varieties of rock.

hill on the right side of the road as you approach the Cape. Among geologists Magerøy is known as a particularly interesting area that shows clearly how these northern outskirts of Europe were built up, with a whole series of rocks lying in the open. They describe the eastern part of the island as a wild, rugged group of mountains, which are replaced towards the west and north-west by a wide plateau about 300 metres over the ocean, partly an even 'table-land', while the middle has many small mountain peaks and little lakes.

Some few animals hold out in this environment, including ptarmigan, hare and otter. Wild mink has found its way out of captivity.

There is a good stock of seabirds, such as gulls, puffins, cormorants, guillemots and auks. Ravens and eagles circle over the nesting-places, whilst the sea around Magerøy teems with the fish that provide the basis for human existence here.

Yrkesfiskeren ved Nordkapp. 　　*The fisherman at work at the Cape.*
Skarp marssol i fiskerhavna. 　　*The fishing port on a sunny day in March.*

SETTLEMENTS

The people live in fishing villages and fishing harbours. They comprise people of Norwegian stock, Sámi people (Lapps), immigrants from Finland, and mixtures of all the three ethnic groups. Originally the fishermen had to build their dwellings as close as possible to the fishing grounds, rowing out in small boats from tiny hamlets like Tunes, Opnan, Helnes, Laukvik and several others. But nobody lives there any more: in modern times, when the fishing boat acquired an engine, people gradually moved in to less stormy surroundings, settling at *Honningsvåg* and similar places.

For a long while *Kjelvik* was the centre of trade and fishing on the eastern side. It was one of the more weatherbeaten places, where the onshore storm winds blew so hard that they damaged the houses. In a furious hurricane in 1882 even the church was blown to pieces; a new church was built on a calmer site at Honningsvåg three years later, and little by little this port replaced Kjelvik as a centre. Today Kjelvik is vacated and Honningsvåg is the town of the island, with about 4000 inhabitants, including the adjacent villages of *Storbukt* and *Nordvågen*. The other surviving prosperous fishing villages are *Kamøyvær* and *Skarsvåg* on the east coast and *Gjesvær* to the west, each with a few hundred inhabitants.

While Storbukt has grown more or less into the neighbouring Honningsvåg, the village of *Nordvågen* lies by itself as the next biggest settlement, five kilometres east of the centre. It is a fishing village in growth, with many new houses and about 700 inhabitants (1978). They have a boat slipway and service station there, a shrimp processing plant and a fishing industry with very advanced equipment. They have also an up-to-date school with a swimming pool and other facilities which provide for spare-time activities like music, athletics, and amateur theatricals.

Kamøyvær lies 'in the middle of the liver' as they say locally,

Pleasure fishing in the midnight sun.

△ *From old Kjelvik.*   ▽ *Honningsvåg seen from the mountain.*

△ *A fine winter day at Nordvågen.*　　　▽ *Storbukt in wintertime.*

Kamøyvær's situation 'in the middle of the liver'.
Kamøyvær – approaches and fishery plant.

which means close to good fishing grounds. It is also beautifully situated, in the bottom of the deep Kamøy fjord, and has a road connection to Honningsvåg. There is a fishing co-operative, a school and a new community house.

Traditionally the men of Kamøyvær use nets for fishing. They are known as 'net specialists', whereas the fishermen of Skarsvåg are longline specialists. Since fish caught by net is not too good for fillet production, the former have kept mainly to the production of salted and dried fish.

Skarsvåg is the first harbour you sight when sailing in from the ocean east of the North Cape. It is usually called the world's northernmost fishing village. The local fishermen 'chug' quickly from here to the grounds near the Cape where they catch most of their fish, for delivery to the modern plant in their home port. Skarsvåg, too, is a growing and well-equipped community.

The village of *Gjesvær*, known from old times as one of the richest fishing stations in the county of Finnmark, lies in a very isolated position on the west coast of the island. A summer road connection to the North Cape was built only in 1976.

Skarsvåg – the most northerly fishing hamlet in the world.

△ *Gjesvær at the foot of Stappene.*

▽ *From the new Gjesvær.*

The settlement originally consisted of a number of small islands with good anchorage in between. Now most of the houses are concentrated on the Gjesværøy. The village has a certain charm and beauty, situated as it is under the 'Stappene', three mountains arising from the sea, also known as 'the Mother and her Daughters'. New houses are still being built in Gjesvær, which has grown into a modern society like the other fishing villages on the island of Magerøy. It possesses a new school with both swimming pool and stage, local shops and other facilities, not to mention three fishing industry plants, so no one now talks about abandoning the place, as they did some years ago.

Then back to *Honningsvåg:* It is today a very busy modern place, sometimes called the world's northernmost urban community (not being in administrative terms a town). This *de facto* town has a thriving industry and trade, its own newspaper, TV in every home, hotels, several schools and a hectic activity in the harbour throughout the year. The fishing industry plants for filleting, freezing, etc., are among the largest in Norway.

Fishery plants at Gjesvær before 1944.

The fact that everybody in town – and on the island – is dependent on the fish of the surrounding sea, is said to give the people a special sense of common feeling and solidarity. Anyway, these people seem to be made of hard stuff; they don't hesitate to try new things and they don't give in easily. As for daily life, you'll find the activities you usually see in Norwegian towns. Football, skiing and indoor swimming are popular sports. Lighted tracks and ski-jumping hills are prepared for the winter. Social life is encouraged through a whole lot of clubs and societies; there is an active film and theatre milieu, and the health service and social security are kept up to welfare state standards. Communications with the outside world by sea and road are fairly good, and an airstrip has recently opened up new possibilities.

THE FISHERIES

Strangely enough, the cold Arctic Ocean seems to provide an agreeable habitat for living creatures of all shapes and sizes. As the local saying has it, the farther north you go, the poorer the country becomes and the richer the sea. The experts explain that the ice-free borders of the Arctic Ocean are so full of plankton that they attract some of the largest schools of fish in the world.

Cod is the foremost species, the North Atlantic cod tribe having its home in the Barents Sea. Each year in January huge schools of cod steer towards the coastal banks to spawn, and many thousand tons of cod are taken ashore at Honningsvåg.

Capelin is a small arctic fish that the young cod pursues in to the coast of Finnmark, which gives the conditions for the large

Net fishing off Magerøy.

Finnmark fisheries. The processing plants in Honningsvåg deal with much of the capelin. The pollack fishing takes place mainly from May to June, and many other species of fish and shellfish for household use are obtained off the coast of Magerøy. Most of the seal and whale, however, were killed off long ago.

Since time immemorial man has harvested the riches of the sea up north. Stone Age man caught the fish on hooks made of bone, rowing out and risking the perils of the sea in skin boats. The whale was chased onto the shore, where he used his spear on it. Seal and polar bear too he attacked with his stone weapons.

The fight against natural forces has always been the challenge to man in these latitudes. Long-lasting storms, winter darkness and cold must be faced before the prey can be hauled in. Man at the edge of the Arctic has been forced to concentrate his strength upon a few areas, in order to make the best possible use of Nature's resources and so survive. Starting with the spear and the skin boat, man gradually developed wooden boats and sails, harpoons and better equipment in general. He managed to create an Arctic culture marvellously adapted to the environment. Boat types and fishing gear bear witness to a high level of cunning and inventiveness.

However, as the boats grew bigger and the tools more sophisticated, man also managed to disturb the balance of nature among his own prey. The big mammals are almost exterminated in the Arctic Ocean. Thousands of fishing boats from countries near and far come to catch the fish here. Their equipment being technically perfect, the fish finds no safe depth to hide in any more. Modern man has the means to empty these rich oceans. The people on Magerøy know all this very well: they must be on the alert and co-operate with other fishing nations to preserve the basis of their existence.

Seine fishing at the North Cape.

△ *The one-man fishing boat still has a future.* ▽ *The assembly belt at the fillet factory.*

What is it like to be a fisherman today? Ask the men who are working out on the North Cape banks, for days without sleep; they will tell you it's still no joke. The fishermen and their families up here have endured hardships through generations. They have not only fought against nature, but against low fish prices, monopolies, exploitation and poverty. Storms and shipwrecks have claimed human lives every year, and still do. Sometimes the big shoals of fish fail to come. Sheep and cattle and agriculture never yielded enough to live on, but fish for dinner was always there, so the fishing family never gave up. A rather tough human type has developed in the fishing villages, now facing new problems of centralization and industrialisation and the claims of the affluent society.

The people of Honningsvåg today are entirely dependent on the modern fishing industry. They produce food for export to many countries: fish meal and oil, frozen fillets and shrimp, and smaller quantities of salted and dried fish.

Fish processing – old style.

△ *A large fish processing plant in Honningsvåg today.*   ▽ *The fishing port in summertim*

They are proud of their harbour, with all its international traffic, which they have developed to serve all kinds of vessels, merchant ships and fishing boats. Scores of foreign ships come to take on board bunkers and provisions, not to mention one of the many coastal pilots stationed here.

British, Polish and Faeroese trawlers are frequent visitors, German, Spanish and Portuguese fishing boats call now and then. Cargo vessels call in on their way to and from the Soviet Union, Honningsvåg being more of a port of call than any other harbour in Northern Norway.

In the tiny town park there is a sculpture of 'The fishing girl' as a symbol of what is going on here, whilst high up on a cliff above the harbour the Fishing Vocational School provides a dominant landmark. The school has courses for fishing skippers, engineers, mechanics, stewards and cooks, and in addition special courses for secondary school pupils.

Inside the new net repair shop.

THE SÁMI PEOPLE – THE LAPPS

The owners of the reindeer you see grazing around on Magerøy have their homes in the Sámi village of Karasjok on the mainland some 200 kilometres to the south. Who are the Sámi people – as the Lapps prefer to be called? Where did they come from, how long have they been using the pastures on Magerøy? Are they the oldest folk-group up here? These questions are more easily asked than answered.

In April-May herds of reindeer counting from four to five thousand head plunge into the cold Magerøy sound, to swim over from the mainland to the summer pastures on the island, having already been driven the long way from their winter pastures near

Reindeer herd swimming the Magerøy sound.

Karasjok Sámi on the quay. ▷

32

Trær vokser normalt ikke på Magerøya; her dyrkes de i hagen i Nordvågen – rogn, hegg, selje, syrin.

No trees grow wild on Magerøy, but this man has planted them in his garden – rowan, bird cherry, sallow, lilac.

Et godt år for molter!

A good season for cloudberries!

Fiskerhavna i vinterdrakt.

Kvinner i filetfabrikken.

Fishing boats in winter.

Women in the filleting plant.

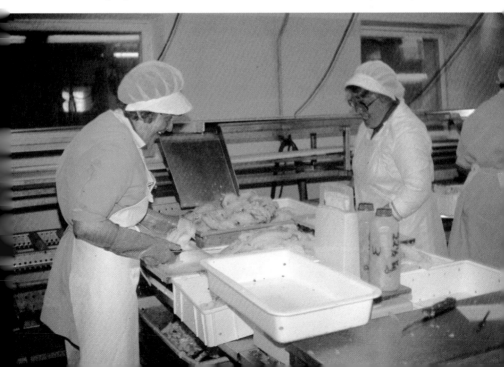

△ *A tourist ship has arrived.*   ▽ *Sámi selling souvenirs at the quay.*

◁ *Reindeer slaughtering.*

3. North Cape

Karasjok. Late in September they are to swim back across the sound again, this time together with the calves born on Magerøy in the spring. The Karasjok Sámi have followed this tradition longer than anybody knows.

Travellers on the road to the North Cape look at the reindeer from their car windows; the Sámi have become a tourist attraction along the road, as well as on the pier in Honningsvåg when the big cruise ships come alongside. They sell souvenirs to the tourists, making a subsidiary income from it, and as a rule the things they offer are real handicraft or art of good quality. The delight in colours and the artistic sense of these mountain people are impressive.

This business is not quite new to them, for the Sámi have been trading with foreign people for centuries, but selling tourist articles does not, of course, belong to the Karasjok Sámi's normal way of life. They have traditions to guard that are not to be influenced by commercial considerations. They belong to a proud and distinctive ethnic group, well aware of their rights as the indigenous

Rounding up reindeer on Magerøy.

people of these regions. Of the folk groups now living here the Sámi are the oldest, and they were using the land long before the Norwegians came here as permanent settlers.

Like the fishermen on the coast the inland Sámi have had to fight against the Arctic climate, against snowstorms and darkness and – in addition – the merciless cold of the inland winter. They have achieved unequalled results in the design of winter dwellings and winter clothing, vehicles, hunting equipment and tools. They have also managed to create remarkable artistic products in skin, bone, wood and wool.

Archaeologists have found traces of people and settlements on the Finnmark coast from ten thousand years back, when the ice melted after the last Ice Age. When the Sámi came in from the east we don't know, nor when they arose as a separate folk group. The first written statement about them is derived from the Norwegian farmer and Viking chief Ottar at the end of the 9th century A.D. Ottar told King Alfred the Great, who had the story recorded, that on sailing along the northern coast from Troms past Finnmark

Near Hornvika the old Sámi once had a place of sacrifice.

and the Kola peninsula, he observed only Sámi people all the way. They are described as hunting for furs and catching seal and fish. In winter they used skis. The Sámi paid tribute to Ottar in furs of bear and marten and skins of reindeer, as well as feathers and down from birds' nests.

Near the creek of Hornvika by the North Cape there was a Sámi place of sacrifice in pre-Christian times, and other holy places of the Sámi are also found on the island. Sámi nature-names are scattered throughout, though seldom printed on a map, names like Saddovarre and Aksonjargga, which show clearly that the Sámi language is entirely different from Norwegian.

The Karasjok people are reindeer Sámi, but only ten per cent of the Sámi live by keeping reindeer; the most usual way of life has been a combination of farming, fishing and hunting. There are some 30–40 000 Sámi in the Northern countries, of whom more than half live in Norway. It is primarily the reindeer-keeping Sámi who carry on the old traditions of Sámi culture.

As a minority the Sámi people have not been well treated, having in many respects suffered a similar fate to that of minorities of indigenous people in other lands, such as the Eskimos or North American Indians. They have been very heavily taxed and looked down upon as a primitive and inferior race, and many of them still feel they are discriminated against in certain ways. This also applies to Magerøy, so that a good many families in Honningsvåg have been reluctant to admit their Sámi origin. But in recent years the Sámi have organised active cultural and political movements; no Sámi is trying to hide his roots any more. Moreover, a good many of them have become integrated in the surrounding Norwegian society, so that today you find people of Sámi blood in all functions on the island, as blue and white collar workers, fishermen and artists.

Welcome to our summer quarters!

A snow scooter has replaced the reindeer in front of the sleigh.

GLIMPSES FROM THE PAST

Famous travellers to the North Cape

At one time or another quite a number of important persons have rounded the Cape, some of whom have written down what they saw. The man who had the honour of naming the place is the British seafarer *Richard Chancellor,* who was driven in his sailing ship close up to the steep cliffs by an onshore storm in the year 1553. He was taking part in Willoughby's Arctic expedition, an unsuccessful attempt to find the North-East Passage to China. Chancellor named the outermost cliff the *North Cape*, the northernmost place he observed in Europe.

Richard Chancellor did achieve something more on the otherwise unfortunate expedition, in which his ship stranded on the shores of the White Sea, for after a time he travelled overland to Moscow, upon the invitation of Czar Ivan IV ('the Terrible'). This led to the trade between Russia and Great Britain conducted by the 'Muscov Company'.

King Christian IV of Denmark-Norway made a voyage to Finnmark in 1599 to inspect the remotest provinces of Norway and determine its borders with Sweden and Russia. He was then a lively young man, very fond of having parties on board. His ship rounded the North Cape in the beginning of the midnight sun season.

The Frenchman *La Martinière* has sketched vividly his journey in a merchant vessel from Copenhagen along the Norwegian coast all the way to the Varanger fiord in 1653.

Some years later, in 1664, the Italian *Francesco Negri* ventured out on a similar journey with a Danish ship to the North Cape and wrote an account of it. In this he expresses his enthusiasm for the scenery of Norway, and calls the North Cape the extreme border of the world.

Another well satisfied Italian, *Giuseppe Acerbi*, travelled

38

Louis Philippe smiles benignly outside the North Cape Hall.

through Sweden and Finland to the North Cape in 1798, and wrote a book about it that came out in London four years later. Acerbi was so proud when he reached the Cape that he said emotionally: I now feel not only as a human being, but as a *creator*.

Some royal travellers have left special memorials of themselves on the North Cape plateau. On a pedestal outside the North Cape Hall a white, pear-shaped face smiles mildly at you: that is *Louis Philippe of Orléans*, later the 'Citizen King' of the French. He was here incognito as an exiled prince in 1795.

A Spanish count and amateur geologist, *Vargas-Bedemar*, was granted royal permission in 1810 to travel from Copenhagen to Norway to investigate geological conditions. He came to Finnmark, and is reported to have mounted with proud steps the cliff of the North Cape.

Xavier Marmier, a well-known French author who travelled all over the world, visited the Northern countries in the years 1836–

Every visitor knows King Oscar's Memorial Stone.

39, and described his visits in a two-volume work in 1841. He was well received on Magerøy and enjoyed the Cape, he writes.

The famous Scottish historian *Thomas Carlyle* (1795–1881) was one of the visitors who were fascinated by the granite green cliffs and the Arctic light at midnight at the North Cape, which was the farthest point he reached.

Another eager traveller to the North Cape was *Prince Napoleon*, a cousin of the Emperor Napoleon III. The Prince came to Norway twice, in 1856 and 1870, the first time on a scientific expedition to the Arctic Ocean.

All later visitors to the plateau have seen the 'Oscar stone', which was erected in memory of *King Oscar II*'s visit in 1873. His ship anchored in Hornvika, and it is reported that the 44-year-old monarch was so light of foot that he trod the steep path to the top without getting out of breath – an example for modern tourists! Before the North Cape Road was opened in 1956 most travellers had to use the path.

The Norway enthusiast *Kaiser Wilhelm II* reached the plateau in 1891 and left a cairn there.

The landmark of North Cape has been regarded more or less as common European property, and many visitors have wanted to leave their mark here. A number of more modest ones are scattered about, including initials carved in stone, such as the King of Siam's from 1907.

Right into the twentieth century to go on a pleasure trip to the North Cape was a privilege confined to the rich. But the effects of the development of affluence in the west have long since reached the Arctic Ocean, and so many ordinary citizens now swarm about that a royal monument or two no longer makes any great impression.

A traditional link with the Russians

How have the relations been between Norway and its big Russian neighbour this far north? Many popular stories are told. Some are about Viking raids to the east and Russian repayments in kind. Then there are stories about skirmishes with Russian pirates on Magerøy in forgotten times. And in our own days we

41

A score of Russian Pomor ships anchored in the bay.

hear of secret submarines and spies, and rumours have it that the Russians are on their way.

The truth seems to be more peaceful. A living tradition about Russians on Magerøy is the *Pomor trade,* which old people still remember; some sounds and anchor places have names related to the trade with the Russians. It was a useful business. The Russian ships were welcomed to the Magerøy fishing villages in spring. It meant, above all, that now the bread meal was secured for the following winter.

The Pomores (from Russian *pomorets* – coastal dweller) were Russian fishing farmers or 'farming skippers' from the White Sea area, who sailed to the coast of Finnmark in summer to barter and buy fish, carrying with them meal, oats, salt and other wares. The fish they needed especially for the many Orthodox fast days they had in Russia then. The Pomor trade flourished from the middle of the 18th century and was regulated in treaties between Russia and Norway, which in 1796 fixed its duration as from 1st July till 15th August. The trade took place on friendly terms in a mixed Norwegian-Russian lingo that both parties understood, and in northernmost Norway the Russian meal was greatly appreciated both in good times and bad. The trade stopped abruptly when the First World War broke out, and although it was taken up again afterwards, it slowly died out after the Russian revolution imposed its ban on private trade.

The North Cape in the Second World War

By the 10th June 1940 the German troops had completed their occupation of Norway. But after the alliance was formed between Great Britain and the Soviet Union in 1941, the big convoys of supplies from Britain to Murmansk and Archangel brought the Finnmark coast into focus for the war at sea. The Germans attacked the convoys with submarines and aircraft from bases on the Norwegian coast, and the convoys suffered heavy losses. In the midnight sun season the attackers could operate day and night, and the situation grew so bad that for a while the convoys had to cease sailing in summer. Operations of war also forced the regular coastal sailings to stop, so that only small freighters covered the traffic from Tromsø to Vadsø after September 1941.

One of those freighters, the *Store Bill* ('Big Bill'), was lying alongside at Honningsvåg on Sunday the 19th July 1942, having arrived from a southern port with 20 tons of potatoes and other cargo. A few days before, a whole fleet of German transport vessels and warships had been in the port, some of which were

Honningsvåg before the war.

43

Honningsvåg after the bombing in 1942.

still lying there, among others a landing barge full of ammunition. The barge was busy at the quay unloading, when the air alarm sounded and Russian bomber planes came sweeping in low over the harbour and attacked. The ammunition barge blew up, as did another boat with explosives farther in. A large part of the houses behind the quays were blown to pieces and many people were killed. After initial rescue work the skipper of the *Store Bill* shifted his vessel to the outer harbour. In the evening the Russians came back, this time so suddenly that there was no time to start the air sirens. The bombs fell shrieking down over the harbour area and the town. Several Norwegian boats were sunk or damaged, including *Store Bill*, which got a direct hit and was set on fire. The whole crew of five were killed, as they were all in the superstructure where the bomb fell.

The wide North Cape area now experienced new and uneasy times. There were just as many submarines and warships to be seen in these waters as freighters and fishing boats; even the tourist ships of peacetime had been converted into troop transport vessels.

Eventually a great naval battle was fought in the far north. At 7 p.m. on Christmas Day 1943 the fast German battlecruiser

Scharnhorst and five destroyers went out from their base in Altafiord to attack an Allied convoy on its way to Murmansk. Somewhere between Bear Island and the North Cape the *Scharnhorst* had contact with the British convoy protection forces and was damaged in an artillery fight. A little later the British battleship *Duke of York* came on the scene together with several destroyers, among them the Norwegian *Stord*, the Allied force being under the command of Admiral Fraser. At 4.50 p.m. on the 26th December a violent exchange of fire broke out in the polar night, in which the *Scharnhorst* was hit by large shells from the battleship and torpedoes from the destroyers, so that it heeled over and went slowly down. The crew jumped overboard in their life jackets, but only 36 men of 1900 were picked up in a one hour's search of the icy waters. For this victory the British admiral was made a peer under the title of 'Baron Fraser of North Cape'. (Later, in 1956, he had the honour of opening the North Cape Road).

For the Finnmark people, the last phase of the war was to be the worst, when they were put to the hardest test. The Germans used 'scorched earth' tactics in Finnmark when retreating before the Soviet troops. They forced the inhabitants to evacuate and burnt down their towns, settlements and farms to the last shack or boathouse. In the autumn of 1944 people in the evacuation boats from Magerøy stood on deck watching clouds of smoke rising from houses all over the island. The Germans destroyed every telephone

Honningsvåg in the spring of 1945 – only the church is left standing.

Honningsvåg, 17th May 1946: the National Day is celebrated among ruins.

pole on Magerøy, whilst in Honningsvåg every house was laid in ashes except the white church.

The people returned home as soon as they could after the liberation. They looked at the burnt-out ruins and talked about how meaningless this burning had proved, since the Russian troops had gone no farther west than the Tana fiord in their pursuit of the Germans. As everywhere in Finnmark, people rolled up their sleeves and started rebuilding their houses with public support. The old fishing milieu with its jetties and boat houses was gone from Honningsvåg for ever, as from other places, but the inhabitants were the same, and they carried on where they had been forced to stop.

EVERYDAY LIFE ON MAGERØY

No one denies that the climate is hard; even the toughest local patriots have their complaints about the weather now and then. Economic experts far down south in the capital may be sitting at their computers wondering: Does it pay to have people living so far north? We must build roads, ports, schools and hospitals in windblown, god-forsaken places that the nation does not need any more. This costs enormous sums of money. How about the national economy?

Fishing boat going out, local ferry coming in.

Waiting for the ferry from the mainland.

The people on Magerøy do not think along such lines; they don't look at the island and their homes as a literally meagre place to live. On the contrary, they say, right outside our door lies one of the richest sea areas in the world, one that for generations has been an important supplier of food for the rest of Europe! Let us live here and take care of the resources in this ocean. We know it best. We have a personal relationship to the waters and the fishing grounds, which representatives of big industry from outside don't have. We won't let the cod disappear like the herring from the North Sea and the whale from the Antarctic.

Other dangers than over-exploitation also threaten the fisheries: how about future oil-boring? This will probably take place in the very areas to which the cod migrates for spawning. Aware as they are of blowouts and pollution, the local fishermen would like to have a vote in this question.

Langs Nordkappveien.   *Along the North Cape Road.*
Midnattssolmarsjen til Nordkapp. *'The Midnight Sun March' to the North Cape.*

Mountain skiing trip on Magerøy at Easter.

Another important resource to be kept up is the reindeer herding, utilising wide pastures which would otherwise lie waste. Five thousand reindeer is a worthwhile business. The old people point to extra incomes from hunting, fishing for home use, picking of blueberries and cloudberries, etc., and the gathering of seabird eggs and down. Once important resources, they still constitute a useful reserve in times of crisis.

The islanders do not want to be remote-controlled from Oslo or other centres. In the referendum in 1972 about Norway joining the EEC, more than 75 % up here voted NO, fearing remote control from Brussels.

Although all the outer fishing stations are abandoned now, the general situation is good. The remaining communities (Hon-

The fishing boat – basis for the Magerøy way of life.

ningsvåg, Kamøyvær, Skarsvåg and Gjesvær) seem to prosper. Modern technique has made it possible for the majority to live well from the fishing industry. The welfare society has come to Magerøy as to the rest of the country. The ordinary family here has a car and its own house of high modern standard. Perhaps they have a cottage too, or they go to Sweden or Finland on a camping holiday. Or they go by air to the Mediterranean or the Canaries.

Indoors, everyday life on Magerøy is very much like that in other Norwegian homes all over the country. The difference is only to be felt climatically. Will this by and by make the people move south and away? At the moment, the islanders don't think so.

Playing in the kindergarten.

50

THE TOURISTS – A PROBLEM?

Some people say: 'The tourists spoil the nature and make the roads noisy all summer; they disturb the grazing of the reindeer; they are a foreign element which destroys the original environment.'

In general, however, all travellers are welcomed to the island. Hotels and shops of course appreciate the stream of tourists. The

People and buses on the plateau.

Outside the Pavilion on the Cape in 1898. The Pavilion later disappeared in a storm.

The opening of the North Cape Road in 1956.

At the furthest goal – the fulfilment of a dream?

North Cape has once and for all become an international attraction, one of the favourite travel targets in the Nordic countries.

The travellers do not go just for the midnight sun, and they do not expect to find summer temperatures here. When the North Cape Road was opened one night shortly after midsummer in 1956, fifteen hundred spectators watched in driving snow and storm squalls. Surely, the tourists seek something more than the pleasure of a beautiful spectacle? Perhaps an outermost destination, the fulfilment of a dream?

The contrast between tourism and working life is certainly present, but should not necessarily mean a strain on relations. However, motorised traffic ought to be cut down a bit. The popular 'North Cape March' – or 'Midnight Sun March' – on foot to the Cape seems to be not a bad idea. Another suggestion is for collective transport: only buses allowed, and a ban on private cars on the North Cape Road. Maybe the northernmost tip of Europe should be, as far as possible, a quiet and protected landmark.